HABIT RESET

Susan Reynolds

BREAK THE CYCLE, BUILD BETTER ROUTINES, AND TAKE BACK CONTROL

chartwell books

Quarto

This edition published in 2026 by Chartwell Books,
an imprint of The Quarto Group
135 W 36th St, Floor 13
New York, NY 10018 USA
T (212) 779-4972
www.Quarto.com

10 9 8 7 6 5 4 3 2 1

ISBN: 978-0-7858-5019-9
Publisher: Wendy Friedman
Publishing Director: Meredith Mennitt
Editor: Joanne O'Sullivan
Designer: Alana Ward
Production Manager: Tom Miller
Image credits: Shutterstock

Printed in Pontian, Johor, Malaysia. PC072026

EEA Representation, WTS Tax d.o.o.,
Žanova ulica 3, 4000 Kranj, Slovenia.
www.wts-tax.si

CONTENTS

WHY IT'S SO HARD TO BREAK BAD HABITS

Our brains process eleven million bits of information every second, but it's estimated that only fifty bits of said information are processed by our conscious minds. Our conscious minds aren't activated unless necessary, so most of the processing and communication happens in our subconscious minds. Well-established habits are 'rote' behaviors that we typically do without thinking; that is, they are activated in our subconscious minds.

In conducting research for the book, *Good Habits, Bad Habits: The Science of Making Positive Changes,* author Wendy Wood found that our actions are habitual 43 percent of the time. This happens because the more we repeat a behavior, the more it becomes rote, which, over time, decreases our tendency to notice what we're doing or change what we consistently do—even when continuing the behavior is detrimental to our mental, physical, or emotional health.

Most of us have made New Year's Resolutions or used our birthday as a starting point to transform our lives by eliminating behaviors that aren't serving us and starting those that would be good for us. We typically start with enthusiasm and perhaps plan for tackling each habit. But often the plans are nebulous and based on willpower. Still, we put our hearts and minds into it . . . for about three weeks.

Then we learn (and relearn and relearn) that effectively and permanently jettisoning ingrained habits and establishing new habits is far from an easy task, and, as humans, we typically want to want to avoid as much discomfort as possible. This is why we gravitate toward whatever 'quick fix' solution someone has proposed to expedite the process. Unfortunately, those 'quick fixes' set you up for failure.

Even those blessed with strong willpower or self-control will find those strengths are not enough to change ingrained habits they want to jettison or reset, nor to sustain new habits they want to establish. To permanently change a habit, you must be conscious, willing, committed, and persistent in repeatedly acknowledging, focusing on, and working through myriad thoughts, feelings, and behaviors that arise—no matter what—in service of breaking bad habits or implementing desirable habits. You need mental focus, preparation, mental, emotional, and physical commitment, and a workable plan that you can and will follow.

If you want to reset your habits, what's required is a three-pillar approach:

1. Understand the Science
2. Create Workable Strategies
3. Maintain the Habits

So, let's dive in by discussing the science, and later we'll get to workable strategies and tips for maintaining the desired habit resets.

"YOUR BELIEFS BECOME YOUR THOUGHTS,
YOUR THOUGHTS BECOME YOUR WORDS,
YOUR WORDS BECOME YOUR ACTIONS,
YOUR ACTIONS BECOME YOUR HABITS,
YOUR HABITS BECOME YOUR VALUES,
YOUR VALUES BECOME YOUR DESTINY."

Mahatma Gandhi

Chapter 1

THE SCIENCE OF HABITS

NEUROPLASTICITY 101

Growing up, we all form 'good habits,' such as brushing our teeth before bed, going to bed at a reasonable hour, eating nutritious breakfasts, focusing when needed at school, and so on. And our brains assist in this habit formation by creating neural pathways that reinforce the facility with which you repeat a behavior. When you've performed the task enough times, the synaptic connections related to the task in your brain are so established, you no longer must think about or pay attention to what you're doing; the behavior becomes an automatic habit.

Sounds great, doesn't it? Unfortunately, there's a catch: Your brain views *all repetitive behavior* as important and does not differentiate between repetitive behaviors you do that are helpful, healthy, or productive versus those that have the opposite effect. Your lovely brain will ingrain the habit that's been created, sustained over time, and with which it's familiar. This is why breaking habits is not an easy task and requires far more time, attention, and effort than simply *deciding not to* do a particular behavior anymore, or even effectively resisting the compulsion to repeat undesired behaviors for a few weeks.

Neuroplasticity Saves the Day

Luckily, your brain also has the capacity for *neuroplasticity,* which is your brain's ability to alter its physical structure, to repair damaged structures, to grow new neurons and discard old ones, to rezone regions that performed one task to have them perform a new task, and to change the circuitry that weaves neurons into the networks that allow us to remember, feel, suffer, think, imagine, and dream.

Here's how neuroplasticity can help you break and establish new habits:

- ❑ It can reactivate long-dormant circuitry. If there was a skill (or habit) you once had, you can restart it by repetitiously stimulating the neurons related to the task.
- ❑ It can create new circuitry. Whenever you learn a new skill (or habit), your brain can strengthen exiting neuronal connections and create new synapses (connections) that allow you to maximize (and deeply ingrain) the new skill (or habit).
- ❑ It can rewire circuitry. Parts of your brain used for one task can be rewired to perform other tasks.
- ❑ It can quiet aberrant circuits and connections. Some parts of your brain can exert control over others and change how they affect your mood, decision-making, and thought processes.

The actions you take can literally expand or contract areas of your brain, For example, if you are susceptible to excessive worrying, your brain has likely created pathways that make worrying second nature. However, if you retrain your brain to quiet those pathways, you can tamp down the neurons that habitually go down the 'worry highway.'

If you habitually feel discouraged when things don't go your way, your brain has reinforced the habit by strengthening neural pathways. If you decide, instead, to avoid your habitual response by focusing instead on creative solutions to address that led to feeling discouraged, you can weaken the neuronal connections that lead to feeling discouraged and increase neuronal connections that foster creativity.

Luckily, your brain is constantly pruning old connections and wiring new ones; and, if you employ *intention, focus, practice, and reinforcement when jettisoning or resetting habits and creating new habits,* your brain will strive to do whatever you want it to do.

"ANY ACT OFTEN REPEATED SOON FORMS A HABIT; AND HABIT ALLOWED, STEADY GAINS IN STRENGTH, AT FIRST, IT MAY BE BUT AS A SPIDER'S WEB, EASILY BROKEN THROUGH, BUT IF NOT RESISTED IT SOON BINDS US WITH CHAINS OF STEEL."

Tyron Edwards

What 'grooves' have formed in your brain ? Are you an excessive worrier, a compulsive eater, a chronic procrastinator? What are eight ingrained habits you have that will require hard work and focus to reset? What makes each reset so difficult? What are the roadblocks?

Habit 1

Habit 2

Habit 3

Habit 4

Habit 5

Habit 6

Habit 7

Habit 8

The Role Your Mind Plays

We are often accustomed to thinking of our brains and our minds as one and the same, but they are not. Both play a role in resetting habits, as does another element of your being—your *self*. Here's the role each plays:

- ❏ Your brain serves as your body's control central. It receives, processes, and coordinates internal and external sensory information and serves as a repository for your memories.
- ❏ Your mind is the element that allows you to be aware of the world and your internal and external experiences in it. Your mind is the locus of consciousness and thought. Without a mind, you wouldn't be able to think or to feel sensations or emotions.
- ❏ Your *self* is your essential being, what distinguishes you from others, and all humans from animals. The self is the locus of introspection, which allows you to reflect upon your being.

If these concepts are hard to grasp, try thinking of your brain as a hardwired motherboard, your mind as the software that contains your working knowledge of the world and determines how those programs interact with each other, and your *self* as the content that the *you* in you types on the screen; the words and thoughts that arise from the interaction of your software (mind) with your motherboard (brain). Your self-created software works in tandem with your brain's hardwired circuitry

When it comes to your conscious thought process, your brain:

- ❏ Takes in sensory information from your internal world and the external world.
- ❏ Uses this information to make conditional rules about the environment.
- ❏ Uses these conditional rules to respond to incoming information by comparing the new information to the preexisting rules.

Your mind, meanwhile:

- Speeds the power of electrical impulses in your brain.
- Keeps you awake and able to consciously process information.
- It keeps your consciousness aware of focused input and uses it to weigh in on the rules your brain is making and to process reactions.
- Provides abstract and complex thinking and helps you make sense of how things are related.
- Provides logic and reasoning across senses and perceptions.
- Contains your *soul.*

The mind and the brain work together bidirectionally. If you make a change in your mind, your brain must also be involved. Your brain functions maintain control of and drive mental activities. However, by employing specific mental activities, you can consciously choose control, drive your brain functions, and create new mental activities and new brain functions.

A Note on The Self

Your autobiographical self (identity/ personality/the *you* in you) is created through experiences and compiled neuron by neuron over time, creating a sort of brain map that your mind uses to form mental images—of your *self* and your world. This *you* in you is flexible. In fact, your brain calls upon its cerebral cortex and its brain stem to stitch together the *you* that you take into the world each day. This ability for your *self* to grow and change plays a crucial role in resetting habits, which we'll discuss in Chapter 2.

"ONCE YOU UNDERSTAND THAT HABITS CAN CHANGE, YOU HAVE THE FREEDOM—AND THE RESPONSIBILITY—TO REMAKE THEM."

Charles Duhigg
The Power of Habit

When it comes to the eight habits you listed on the previous pages as those you would like to reset, how have each affected the *you* in you?

Habit 1

Habit 2

Habit 3

Habit 4

Habit 5

Habit 6

Habit 7

Habit 8

What would the 'top five' of the habits you listed that you want to reset?

1. ____

____

2. ____

____

3. ____

____

4. ____

____

5. ____

____

Think It and It Will Come

Neuroscientific studies have shown that your brain can reshape itself and form new synapses purely from thinking thoughts. Not only does what you think about and how you think really matter, but your thoughts can create new realities. If you can envision something thoroughly and often enough, it can come. This will help you solidify new habits by thinking long and hard about why you want to change them, how to change them, and how doing so will change how you think about yourself.

"GREATNESS IS THE RESULT OF VISIONARIES WHO PERSEVERE, FOCUS, BELIEVE, AND PREPARE. IT IS A HABIT, NOT A BIRTHRIGHT."

Lewis Howes

Pause briefly to think about the ingrained habits you want to jettison, reset, or create. To keep it manageable, work with your top five habits that need to be reset or established. Consider why you want to do so and how you think focusing on these habits will improve your life. Be as specific as possible, as this will be the first step in successful habit resetting.

Habit 1

Habit 2

Habit 3

Habit 4

Habit 5

Don't Wait for Motivation

When launching a reset, it's common to assume you need to feel sufficient motivation to set your efforts in motion. Neuroscientist Yuji Ikegaya says one should not wait to feel motivated. "You won't feel motivated unless you start acting. You feel motivated when the nucleus accumbens in the brain functions, but it doesn't function unless you start doing something." Thus, the only way to gin up motivation is to get started and take responsibility for taking all actions required to reset your habits.

The Hardest Habits to Break

Breaking any habit is not necessarily easy. Routines can become hardwired in our brains, producing the dopamine rush that feels so good. This reward cycle keeps us craving the things we're trying so hard to resist. It takes clarification, commitment, time, effort, repetition, accountability, and persistence.

- ❑ **Smoking and Vaping:** Nicotine is highly addictive. If you've been smoking or vaping for a long time, your body has developed a physical dependency. It will require substantial effort and persistence over a long period of time to break the habit. In addition to battling the addiction, triggers to smoke are likely very present in your life. You will have to make major environmental adjustments to curb urge to smoke.
- ❑ **Excessive Alcohol Consumption:** Like smoking, if you habitually (almost daily or daily) consume large amounts of alcohol, your body has likely developed a dependency that can take years to diminish. It may well be necessary to hire professional help and to join a support group.
- ❑ **Screen Time/Doomscrolling:** Cell phones, tablets, and computers were so much fun when we first acquired them. Little did we realize how quickly being overly attached to being on your phone, scrolling social media multiple times a day, or jumping every time you get a notification becomes addictive. There are, however, some simple environmental changes you can make (which we discuss on pages 000 to 000) that will help.
- ❑ **Emotional/Unhealthy Eating:** When overeating or eating too many processed foods, saturated fats, or sugar is triggered by your emotions, the habit is likely so ingrained that it will also take a huge effort to reset it. Probing the origins of when you first began using

food to quiet your emotions is a good strategy, as is learning better ways to feel, process, and release emotions.

- ❏ **Procrastination:** Even though it produces a lot of stress or anxiety, procrastinators usually have a deep-rooted fear of being inadequate and/or an obsession with perfectionism that overrules the stress and anxiety. Both of those mindsets are hard to change. You'll need to address the fear behind your hesitancy and slowly reset your procrastination habit by creating and meeting a strict timeline.
- ❏ **Negative Self-Talk:** If you're someone who habitually practices self-criticism, this is also a deeply ingrained mental habit that is hard to break.

Why Willpower Isn't Enough

Because you're fighting hard-wired behavior that has its own set of unconscious cues that set a desire in motion, designing how your daily environment functions trumps 'trying harder.' Studies have found that as the strength of a habit grows, intention becomes decreasingly predictive of the behavior. That's why even when you intend to change behavior, because of all the ongoing processes related to how your brain functions, it's not enough to reset your habits.

To successfully reset habits, you must consciously and proactively commit to incrementally doing things differently than you had before. Then, you must ritualistically practice the habit for a minimum of two months or three months. Resetting habits is all about utilizing conscious choice to subvert, redirect, or reinforce unconscious, automatic behavior.

What habits have you tried unsuccessfully to break in the past? Why do you think you weren't able to successfully reset those habits?

"STRENGTHENING NEURAL SYSTEMS IS NOT FUNDAMENTALLY DIFFERENT [THAN STRENGTHENING CERTAIN MUSCLE GROUPS THROUGH PHYSICAL EXERCISE]. IT'S BASICALLY REPLACING CERTAIN HABITS OF MIND WITH OTHER HABITS."

Richard Davidson, Ph.D.

Embrace Your Mental and Emotional Strengths

There's far more to resetting habits that understanding how your brain works. While that is crucial, recognizing and making use of your mental and emotional strengths will play a significant role in the resetting process. Here are a few that you likely possess and will need to call forward:

1. **Emotional resiliency:** You're aware of the role emotions play in triggering behaviors, and you're confident you can recognize when your emotions are sabotaging your efforts and that you will utilize your ability to manage your emotions.
2. **Grit:** When you're knowledgeable and passionate about what matters most to you, what you want, what's required, and what you're willing to do to achieve your goals, all of which reveal the mental fortitude required to reset habits.
3. **Patience and Self-Control:** You recognize that resetting habits will take time, patience, repetition, and commitment. Awareness of the process will help you put in the time required and consistently choose self-control to push you forward.
4. **Motivation:** You set goals, create strategies for achieving them, and make an unwavering commitment that drives you forward. This ability to motivate yourself serves to keep you on track.
5. **Self-Awareness:** You know what matters most to you, what throws you off course, how it feels when you're not being accountable, and how it feels to succeed, all of which will help you stay on course.
6. **Ability to Focus:** You recognize the importance of focusing on your personal goals and repeatedly committing to working towards them.
7. **Bouncing back from 'failure':** You learned long ago that 'failure' is neither permanent nor a personality trait. It simply means that you need to try a new approach.
8. **Positive Mindset:** You don't let setbacks affect your determination or confidence that you are going forward and will succeed.

Which of the strengths you listed previously come easy for you? How have they helped you break or form new habits in the past?

Are there any of the strengths you listed that you need to fortify? What will be required to bolster them?

"YOUR HABITS ARE THE SILENT ARCHITECTS OF YOUR LIFE."

Colby Kultgen

HOW HABITS FUNCTION

Habits are the thoughts, feelings, and behaviors you likely repeat daily, mostly without thinking or perhaps even noticing. They reflect what you learned to do in certain situations and that you repeated so often that your brain has created directional pathways to make your habits even easier to do without noticing that you're doing them. Most habits occur subconsciously as a default response.

Luckily, how habits function is relatively simple to understand, and thereby extremely helpful in resetting bad habits that don't serve you into good habits that will improve your life and bring you closer to the life you want.

Cue or Trigger: This is whatever triggers the behavior or action and then instructs your brain to automatically do what you always do. Cues could be a feeling, a sight, a smell, a time of day, what someone says to you, or what your taste buds crave. Resetting habits will require identifying the cues that set them in motion so you can consciously choose to adopt the new habit you are creating in its place and continue to do so until the new habit becomes deeply ingrained.

Response/Habitual Behavior: This is the thought, emotion, behavior, or action the cue sets in motion. The trigger leads you to do predetermined actions or what you typically do in, without thinking, planning, or choosing. When it's an ingrained habit your response happens automatically—unless you intervene.

Reward: When your brain receives a reward for the behavior or action you've just taken, it decides whether it should become 'routine' based on the reward. The reward comes when you feel happy or joyful, which bathes your brain in dopamine, widely referred to as the 'happy chemical.' The more you repeat the action, the stronger the link between the action and the reward your brain desires. Over time, with repetition, your dendritic spine, the portion of your brain that receives signals, and responds by sending nerve cells to execute the behavior or action, increases in size.

Just to get acquainted with the process, identify the top five habits you'd like to reset, then identify the cue, response, and reward for each.

Habit #1 ______________________________

____

Cue:

____

____

____

____

____

Response/Habitual Behavior:

____

____

____

____

____

Reward:

____

____

____

____

____

____

Habit #2 ______________________________

Cue:

Response/Habitual Behavior:

Reward:

Habit #3 ______________________________

____

Cue:

____

____

____

____

____

Response/Habitual Behavior:

____

____

____

____

____

Reward:

____

____

____

____

____

____

____

Habit #4 ______________________________

____

Cue:

____

____

____

____

____

Response/Habitual Behavior:

____

____

____

____

____

Reward:

____

____

____

____

____

____

____

Habit #5 ______________________________

____

Cue:

____

____

____

____

____

Response/Habitual Behavior:

____

____

____

____

____

Reward:

____

____

____

____

____

____

____

Most Habits Have Common Triggers or Cues

Triggers are often connected to one of the four circumstances listed below:

1. Location
2. Time
3. Emotional state
4. Preceding event

Again, using the five priority habits you previously identified, which of the four triggers you listed set off the habits you'd like to reset? Use the following pages to identify your triggers and set out a plan to overcome them.

Beware Regret

According to Fumio Sasaki, author of *Hello, Habits,* emotions play a key role in resetting habits. When you fail to either stop the 'bad' habit or to execute the 'desired' habit, you spend more time regretting your slip than suffering the actual consequences. Also, when you succeed at executing the habit, the serotonin levels in your brain flood your brain with happy chemicals. Also, Sasaki reported, when your serotonin levels are high, it's easier for you to wait for a reward.

Habit #1 ______________________ **is triggered by:** ___________________________

____

How did the connection form? How will it make the habit harder to reset?

____

____

____

____

____

____

____

____

____

How can you overcome this?

____

____

____

____

____

____

____

____

____

Habit #2____________________ **is triggered by:**____________________

How did the connection form? How will it make the habit harder to reset?

How can you overcome this?

Habit #3____________________ is triggered by:____________________

How did the connection form? How will it make the habit harder to reset?

How can you overcome this?

Habit #4____________________ **is triggered by:** ____________________

____

How did the connection form? How will it make the habit harder to reset?

____

____

____

____

____

____

____

____

____

How can you overcome this?

____

____

____

____

____

____

____

____

____

Habit #5____________________ **is triggered by:**____________________

____

How did the connection form? How will it make the habit harder to reset?

How can you overcome this?

Every Habit Has an Underlying Purpose

Although it may not be obvious, all ingrained, often unconscious, behaviors became habits because each served an underlying purpose. It could have been something you did to relieve stress, a source of comfort, a way to distract yourself from something difficult or painful, or simply something that you found pleasant or entertaining.

Again, think about the five habits you identified as those you want to reset and then identify each one's purpose.

Habit #1:

Habit #2:

Habit #3:

Habit #4:

Habit #5:

"A GROWING BODY OF RESEARCH SUGGESTS THAT AS LITTLE AS FIVE PERCENT OF OUR BEHAVIORS ARE CONSCIOUSLY SELF-DIRECTED. WE ARE CREATURES OF HABIT AND AS MUCH AS NINETY-FIVE PERCENT OF WHAT WE DO OCCURS AUTOMATICALLY OR IN REACTION TO A DEMAND OR AN ANXIETY."

Jim Loehr

Every Habit Has a Hidden Reward

Hidden rewards are the not-easily-identified goodies a habit provides. A procrastinator, for example, receives the 'hidden reward' of not producing work that has the potential to be criticized or judged.

Someone who compulsively exercises may be receiving the hidden reward of feeling a false sense of control. Someone who habitually turns down all social invitations may think they're protecting themselves. But the hidden reward may be that keeping a distance between themselves and others secretly helps them feel superior.

Referring to the same five habits, what are the 'hidden' rewards behind the habits you want to reset?

Habit #1: ______________________________

Do these hidden rewards give you a false sense of control? A license to fail? How can you combat the hidden rewards?

____

____

____

____

____

____

____

____

____

____

Habit #2: ____________________

Do these hidden rewards give you a false sense of control? A license to fail? How can you combat the hidden rewards?

Habit #3: ____

Do these hidden rewards give you a false sense of control? A license to fail? How can you combat the hidden rewards?

Habit #4:____________________________________

Do these hidden rewards give you a false sense of control? A license to fail? How can you combat the hidden rewards?

Habit #5:____

Do these hidden rewards give you a false sense of control? A license to fail? How can you combat the hidden rewards?

"IF YOU ARE GOING TO ACHIEVE EXCELLENCE IN BIG THINGS, YOU DEVELOP THE HABIT IN LITTLE MATTERS. EXCELLENCE IS NOT AN EXCEPTION; IT IS A PREVAILING ATTITUDE."

Colin Powell

Rewards Are Essential

When resetting habit your brain needs to experience an actual reward; otherwise, the replacement habit is not likely to stick. The more you practice the new habit, and reward yourself in a healthy fashion, the sooner your brain will form the synaptic connections that eventually help the new habit become something you habitually do without thinking. Repeated practice also helps your brain develop a craving for that specific reward (which should only happen when you execute the new habit). Rewarding yourself with a hot bath, a cup of your favorite tea, or listening to your favorite song are all healthy options, but the reward doesn't have to be something tangible.

When fully recognized and appreciated, a surge of the brain's 'happy chemicals' (dopamine and endorphins) can become sufficient reward. Even consciously recognizing and feeling a sense of accomplishment can serve as a reward. For example, simply noting that the habit you're resetting will bolster your overall health and pausing to feel proud of yourself can be sufficient reward.

Just be sure to attach the reward to the desired behavior and be conscious when executing or noticing the reward.

"CHANGING YOUR ACTIONS IN ORDER TO FORM A NEW HABIT WITHOUT ALSO CHANGING WHO YOU ARE BEING IS LIKE RUNNING INTO THE WIND: YES, IT'S POSSIBLE TO PUT YOUR HEAD DOWN, RUN AS HARD AS YOU CAN, AND GAIN SOME GROUND, BUT YOU'RE MUCH MORE LIKELY TO GIVE UP AND RETURN TO YOUR OLD WAYS THAN IF YOU RUN IN THE SAME DIRECTION AS THE WIND."

Jen Sincero
Badass Habits

"WHEN YOU MAKE THE RIGHT CHOICES—HOWEVER SMALL—AND DO IT CONSISTENTLY OVERTIME, IT CAN MAKE A HUGE DIFFERENCE IN YOUR LIFE. IF YOU REMEMBER WHY YOU'RE MAKING THOSE CHOICES, IT BECOMES EASIER."

John C. Maxwell,
The 15 Invaluable Laws of Growth

Chapter 2

STRATEGIES FOR RESETTING HABITS

STRATEGIES FOR RESETTING HABITS

The first step in resetting habits is, of course, to identify the habits you want to curtail and those you want to adopt. We're going to discuss the different kinds of habits in this chapter and address how to reset them in the next chapter, so for now, make a list of the habits you want to reset or jettison. You can start with the five you identified in Chapter 1 or create a new list. The five habits I want to establish, reset, or eliminate and *the reasons why* are:

Habit #1:

Habit #2:

Habit #3:

Habit #4:

Habit #5:

The habits I could adopt to replace the habits I chose:

Habit #1:

Habit #2:

Habit #3:

Habit #4:

Habit #5:

Keystone Habits

Keystone habits are habits that set a series of habits in motion. This happens because the actions are linked together. When your alarm buzzes, turning it off leads to getting out of bed, taking a shower, drying your hair, applying makeup or shaving, and getting dressed, all habits that have become routine and thus can be activated by the keystone habit of turning off your alarm.

What are your keystone habits? Which ones work very well, and which do you need to adjust? Which ones affect the top five habits you want to reset?

____

____

____

____

____

Healthy Habits Can Be Calming

Heathy habits or routines that you commonly do can help calm your nervous system. If you've had a bad day, but you do what you always do, it can calm your mind and change your mood. Doing your regular routine restores your nervous system to your normally 'calm state.' The negative mood subsides both because you calmed your system and because it feels good to practice healthy habits.

Lead Domino Habits

Lead Domino habits that set a chain of habitual behavior you are seeking to reset in motion. This chain of habits doesn't necessarily go in a certain order; the lead domino just sets the backsliding in motion. For example, your domino could be skipping your workout, which leads to deciding may as well eat that donut, and have a cheeseburger for lunch, and nibble on chips later.

What are your lead domino habits?

What sets them in motion?

Which are the most problematic?

"TRAINING YOUR BRAIN IS LIKE TRAINING A DOG TO SIT OR COME OR GO LIE DOWN. IT'S ALL ABOUT MEANING, SIMPLICITY, TREATS, AND REPETITION."

Jen Sincero

Badass Habits

In pondering the top five habits you want to reset, what are lead domino habits that could sabotage each and how can you counteract them?

Habit#1

Habit #2:

Habit #3:

Habit #4:

Habit #5:

"THE SECRET TO PERMANENTLY BREAKING ANY BAD HABIT IS TO LOVE SOMETHING GREATER THAN THE HABIT."

Bryant McGill

Emotional Triggers

Identify the emotions behind undesirable habits: loneliness, sadness, stress, boredom, frustration, disappointment. These habits are harder to break without first addressing the emotions that set them in motion.

List the habits you want to reset, then identify the emotions or incidents that trigger your habits.

Habit #1:

____

____

____

____

____

____

Habit #2:

____

____

____

____

____

____

Habit #3:

Habit #4:

Habit #5:

Are You an Emotional Eater?

Many of us learned to quiet upsetting emotions with food, which can throw a real monkey wrench into resetting eating habits. Consider the following:

Does your hungry come on quickly or gradually?

Do you crave specific foods or food groups (salty, sweet, bread)?

Does the hunger start in your stomach or your mind?

Do you feel miserable, ashamed, or guilty after you satisfy a food craving or overindulge?

Emotional eating often comes on quickly, and from your mind (or feelings), sets off a craving, and makes you feel like you've been weak-willed or 'bad,' particularly if you overindulge.

Strategies for Emotional Eaters

Before you give in to a sudden craving or clearly know that your desire to eat something you shouldn't eat, try these strategies for resetting habits:

- ❑ Pause to rate your hunger on a scale of 1 to 10. Can you wait longer?
- ❑ Check in with your emotions: Are you feeling scared, sad, angry, stressed, exhausted? Sit with the emotion, mindfully meditate for 5 minutes on what may be causing the feeling.
- ❑ What else could you try to quiet the feelings behind your sudden hunger or craving? Ask yourself what you need to feel better (other than food).
- ❑ Do something else right away: take a walk, call a friend, clean your house. Choose something active, then reward yourself (but not with food!).
- ❑ Work on making healthy food choices your comfort food.

The Five-Reasons Strategy

It's often hard to pinpoint why you indulge habits that clearly cause self-harm, such as eating too much sugar, staying up late, overcrowding your schedule, and so on. Here's a simple way to nail it down: Write a least five reasons you can think of that you continue a habit that isn't serving you. Avoid the easy answers, and 'dig deep' within your psyche, perhaps back to childhood, to identify the root cause. This may take time and unearth emotions you would rather not face, however, once you find the root cause, the work to get there will make it easier to first own, then reset undesirable, unhealthy, and nonproductive habits.

Even highly functionable, beneficial habits can have a cost. Before we launch into strategies, pause to think about the cost for each of the habits you identified.

What's the price you pay for each of the habits you listed? How will the price affect you over the next five years, ten years?

Habit #1: ______________________________

Habit #2: ______________________________

Habit #3: ______________________

Habit #4: ______________________

Habit #5: ______________________________

Scale Down Your Habits

Often the habits we want to change are so deeply ingrained and so complex that successfully resetting them seems impossible. A strategy is to scale down a habit until it's impossible for you to say 'no.' Think of the scaled-down habits as micro-habits, or very small actions that take little time and effort. They are designed to be easy enough that you don't form excuses to skip them. They can also be used when a new habit is too broad. So, instead of addressing it head-on, try breaking off a piece and change that first, then scale up until you can make the final 'big' reset.

EXAMPLES OF MICRO-HABITS INCLUDE:

- ❏ Drinking a glass of water upon waking to hydrate your body and mind.
- ❏ Writing down three things you're grateful for each day.
- ❏ Doing a three-minute meditation before work to increase your ability to focus.
- ❏ Repeating an affirmation each day to improve your mood.
- ❏ Smiling at yourself in the mirror to boost self-compassion.

HOW TO GET STARTED WITH MICRO HABITS

1. Choose one tiny action. Start with a habit so small it feels impossible to fail.
2. Anchor your habit. Attach your micro habit to something you already do.
3. Be specific and realistic.
4. Track your progress and celebrate wins.

Of the habits you identified earlier that you want to reset, break each one down into micro-components. Identify the micro-habits for each and then choose the micro-habit you can more easily address to get your habit resets started.

Habit #1: ______________________________

Micro-habits: ______________________________

____

____

____

____

Micro-habit to focus on: ______________________________

____

____

____

____

____

Habit #2: ______________________________

Micro-habits: ______________________________

____

____

____

____

Micro-habit to focus on: ______________________________

____

____

____

____

Habit #3: ______________________________

Micro-habits: ______________________________

____

____

____

____

Micro-habit to focus on: ______________________________

____

____

____

____

____

Habit #4: ______________________________

Micro-habits: ______________________________

____

____

____

____

Micro-habit to focus on: ______________________________

____

____

____

____

Habit #5: ______________________________

Micro-habits: ______________________________

Micro-habit to focus on: ______________________________

Micro-habits offer opportunities to more easily create 'wins,' the mental, emotional, or physical reward you feel when you've practiced the new habit. Each of these micro-wins can generate dopamine hits for your brain, which reinforces the desire to stay on track.

Another option is to take minimum viable action. If you simply cannot motivate yourself to put on workout clothes and drive to the nearest gym, try putting on your walking shoes and taking a spin around the block. Taking these kinds of micro-steps and reaping the rewards will give you fuel for tackling more resets.

Use the space below to report your progress in trying micro-habits.

"THE COGNITIVE REVOLUTION LED PEOPLE TO FOCUS ON MOTIVATION, GOALS, COGNITIVE PRACTICES, HOW PEOPLE THINK. BUT WE'RE FINALLY SEEING THE LIMITS OF THOUGHTS AND FEELINGS, AND WE'RE STARTING, AS A DISCIPLINE, TO REALIZE THAT HOW PEOPLE ACTUALLY ACT DAY IN, DAY OUT IS ALSO QUITE IMPORTANT."

Wendy Wood, Ph.D.,

Good Habits, Bad Habits: The Science of Making Positive Changes That Stick

How to Make Healthy Habits A Lifetime Pursuit

Eating healthy and being physically active are lifelong behaviors, not one-time events. To make permanent, ongoing changes, you'll need to keep things interesting, avoid slip-ups, and find ways to cope with what life throws at you. Here are some tips:

ADD VARIETY AND STAY MOTIVATED:

- ❏ Mix up your routine with new physical activities and goals, new physical activity buddies, new foods, tasty recipes, and satisfying rewards.

DEAL WITH UNEXPECTED SETBACKS:

- ❏ Plan ahead to avoid setbacks. For exercise, have a bad weather plan, an injury plan, or ideas for dealing with other issues that might arise. For eating healthier, plan ahead for how you'll deal with traveling or dining out, like packing healthy snacks while on the road or sharing an entrée with a friend in a restaurant.
- ❏ Setbacks are part and parcel of the process. Don't waste time beating yourself up, simply regroup and focus on meeting your goals again as soon as you can.

CHALLENGE YOURSELF:

- ❏ Revisit your goals and think of ways to expand them. For example, if you're comfortable walking five days a week, consider adding strength training twice a week. If you have successfully cut back on saturated fats, work on cutting back on sugar. Small changes can lead to healthy habits worth keeping.

"THE MORE WE BUILD HABITS AROUND WHAT REALLY MATTERS, THE MORE THE RESULTS AND BENEFITS OF THOSE HABITS ADD UP."

Greg McKeown

"THE REAL REASON WHY HABITS MATTER IS BECAUSE LEARNING NEW HABITS IS THE ONLY WAY GO FROM WHAT YOUR DAY-TO-DAY LIFE LOOKS LIKE RIGHT NOW TO THE LIFE YOU WANT."

Mel Robbins

Chapter 3

MY HABIT RESET

MY HABIT RESET

Resetting habits is not easy and often not successful over the long term. You can significantly increase your chances of successfully resetting habits if you first develop a detailed strategy unique to the habit reset. Think about a specific habit you want to reset, then answer the fourteen questions over the following pages.

What are the habit you want to reset?

Habit #1

Habit #2

Habit #3

Habit #4

Habit #5

What cues or triggers set it in motion?

Habit #1

Habit #2

Habit #3

Habit #4

Habit #5

How do each of the habits manifest in your life?

Habit #1

Habit #2

Habit #3

Habit #4

Habit #5

Approximately when did each habit begin?

Habit #1

Habit #2

Habit #3

Habit #4

Habit #5

Were there any relevant circumstances that contributed to the habit formation?

Habit #1

Habit #2

Habit #3

Habit #4

Habit #5

Have the habits changed over time? If so, how?

Habit #1

Habit #2

Habit #3

Habit #4

Habit #5

What time of day do you typically engage in the habitual behavior?

Habit #1

Habit #2

Habit #3

Habit #4

Habit #5

Is the habit related to a specific location or situation?

Habit #1

Habit #2

Habit #3

Habit #4

Habit #5

Are there any triggering people, events, or circumstances that typically occur?

Habit #1

Habit #2

Habit #3

Habit #4

Habit #5

Does the habit affect other people or facets of your life?

Habit #1

Habit #2

Habit #3

Habit #4

Habit #5

What does the habit do for you? Note that this may not be obvious, as it may be something that sabotages efforts in a way that protects you. If you have trouble figuring out why you began this habit and what it does for you, see 'Five-Reasons Strategy' on page 82.

Habit #1

Habit #2

Habit #3

Habit #4

Habit #5

How happy (or unhappy) are you as result of this habit? What rewards or punishment do you experience?

Habit #1

Habit #2

Habit #3

Habit #4

Habit #5

What new habit would you like to create to replace this habit?

Habit #1

Habit #2

Habit #3

Habit #4

Habit #5

How could you set the new habit in motion?

Habit #1

Habit #2

Habit #3

Habit #4

Habit #5

Now that you've explored each habit in depth, the second step in your strategizing is to break down the habit loop by identifying the habit's cue, how it regularly manifests, and how it provides some sort of reward. This will help you to become very familiar with the habit, how it functions, and why you continue doing it. Then, using that information, you can begin making changes you seek to make.

Habit #1

What is the habit?

What is the cue?

What is the routine?

What is the reward?

Habit #2

What is the habit?

What is the cue?

What is the routine?

What is the reward?

Habit #3

What is the habit?

What is the cue?

What is the routine?

What is the reward?

Habit #4

What is the habit?

What is the cue?

What is the routine?

What is the reward?

Habit #5

What is the habit?

What is the cue?

What is the routine?

What is the reward?

Because a habit becomes a pathway that your brain automatically follows, the best way to reset or re-engineer the current habit loop is to create a new habit loop to replace the one you're seeking to alter or eliminate. In the spaces on the these pages, identify the replacement habit you will adopt and answer the following questions:

Habit #1

What is the habit?

What is the cue?

What is the routine?

What is the reward?

Habit #2

What is the habit?

What is the cue?

What is the routine?

What is the reward?

Habit #3

What is the habit?

What is the cue?

What is the routine?

What is the reward?

Habit #4

What is the habit?

What is the cue?

What is the routine?

What is the reward?

Habit #5

What is the habit?

What is the cue?

What is the routine?

What is the reward?

Check Your Environment

One of the first strategies to employ is removing as much temptation or cues from your environment. How does your living environment (physical, emotional, social) affect the possibility of resetting the habit? Would it be possible for you to limit the amount of unhealthy food that comes in the house? Can you keep a journal by your bed to encourage you to track your progress? When focused on resetting a habit, remember these two principles related to designing a conducive, supportive environment:

- ❑ Make it harder to automatically resort to the undesirable habit. Don't bring cookies or baked goods into your home!
- ❑ Make it easier to choose the new habit. Stock up on healthy snacks!

Look around your home or workspace and identify anything that assists in sustaining the habits you want to reset. List them below and then ponder how you can counteract them.

"WE CAN'T BREATHE IN THE FUTURE, AND WE CAN'T BREATHE IN THE PAST. WE CAN ONLY BREATHE IN THE MOMENT, SO AWARENESS OF BREATH KEEPS US FOCUSED ON WHERE WE ARE IN THE PRESENT. IF WE GET CAUGHT UP IN WORRY, DOUBT, FEAR, OR MEMORIES, THE COMING BACK TO THE BREATH BREAKS THE TRAIN OF THOUGHT AND CREATES A GAP WHERE AWARENESS CAN OCCUR."

Michael Bernard Beckwith

Never Miss Twice

Make yourself a promise that you won't let one slip up stop your momentum. Decide now that any misses are not a reason to give up, but rather a sign that you need to redouble your efforts. Simply never allow yourself to miss repeating the habit two days in a row.

If you miss the desired action for new habit formation, what will you do to immediately reset? For example, if the slip was failing to show up for work on time, you'd perhaps set an earlier time to leave your house the next day.

Find a Supportive Network: Elicit help from supportive friends or family who won't nag but will encourage and cheer when you succeed.

- ❑ Is there someone in your life who wants you to keep the habit? Is there a way it benefits them, even as it costs you? Does your thin sister appear happier and more secure when you're carrying 20 extra pounds? Does your boyfriend secretly like it when you constantly look to him for help with something you could handle on your own?
- ❑ Are there people or situations that make it difficult to reset? To secure or thank you for your help, do coworkers bring in irresistible donuts? When you don't want to hang out at night or want to go home early, do your friends call you a 'buzz kill' to make you stay?

Who might consciously or unconsciously sabotage your efforts to change you habits? How and why does this occur? How can you counteract it?

____

____

Who could serve as your support network? Why and how could they help?

____

____

"TAKE NOTE OF WHO'S WHO AND WHAT'S WHAT IN YOUR LIFE. THE PEOPLE, THE HABITS, THE DIET, THE ROUTINES . . . ARE THEY DRIVING YOU FORWARD OR CRAZY?"

Steve Maraboli

Set Boundaries

Boundaries are internal and external limits you set for yourself. The internal ones are vows you make to yourself not to cross a particular line, or repeat a bad habit, or fail to practice a replacement habit. Basically, it's practicing self-discipline. Think of the boundaries you set as self-care. Some might be:

- ❏ I won't allow myself to get so cranked up before bedtime that I can't sleep. Instead, I'll take a hot bath, give myself a facial, or read for 30 minutes.
- ❏ I won't allow myself to scroll on my phone for two hours. Instead, I'll give myself 15 minutes, then do some gentle stretches or watch my favorite show.
- ❏ I won't buy unhealthy treats at the supermarket. I'll buy fruit instead!
- ❏ When I slide backwards, I won't berate or punish myself; I'll simply go forward.

Let's go back to the five habits you are seeking to reset. What internal boundaries do you need to set for each and what new behavior could replace the habit you're wanting to abate?

Habit #1 ______________________________

____

____

____

____

____

____

Habit #2 ____

____

____

____

____

____

Habit #3 ____

____

____

____

____

____

Habit #4 ____

____

____

____

____

____

Habit #5 ____

____

____

____

____

External boundaries are limits you set as to how others treat you. Basically, it's what you can and cannot tolerate without feeling taken advantage of, disrespected, sabotaged, criticized, angry, hurt, and so on. Signs that you need to set external boundaries:

- ❏ You feel taken advantage of (ripped off, resentful) by someone or some situation.
- ❏ You feel disrespected, insulted, or hurt by something someone says or does.
- ❏ You are being blamed for things that are not your fault.
- ❏ Your privacy is constantly interrupted; your time is not respected.
- ❏ You feel pressured to think, do, or say things that don't sit right with you.
- ❏ You feel bullied or abused.

Again, let's review the five habits you are seeking to reset. Simply list them (and replacement habits) in the space provided, then consider them as you ponder what external boundaries you need to set.

Habit #1 ______________________________

____

____

____

____

____

____

____

____

____

Habit #2 ______________________________

Habit #3 ______________________________

Habit #4 ______________________________

Habit #5 ______________________________

Common Boundary Issues

Most of may not even be aware of setting boundaries. We don't give much thought to them until a blatant breach occurs and we realize we need to establish parameters for engagement. Oddly enough, we all have common boundary issues, such as:

1. **We say 'yes' when we'd rather say 'no.'** Maybe you don't want to disappointment someone, or perhaps you fear confrontation. You may also be afraid of appearing selfish or think that being accommodating makes you important to the other person.
2. **We say 'no' far too often.** Maybe you are afraid that letting others get to know you will lead to them not liking you so avoid social invitations or opportunities to get closer to someone. You may have gotten so used to saying 'no' that you don't even realize how much you are denying yourself experiences.
3. **We get enmeshed.** Without boundaries, it's easy to get entangled in each other's lives, to the point where we become more concerned about someone else's emotions than our own. This 'meddling' becomes unhealthy, particularly if you are trying to control someone else's behavior or getting so involved in their lives that you avoid dealing with your own.

While you may think setting boundaries could be viewed as rude, in truth, setting boundaries is a way to show respect to yourself—and others. People like having parameters and they will ultimately respect you more for setting limits. Boundaries are simply a way to say what you do or do not prefer or are willing to accept.

Identify each person or situation that is causing your distress. Write about each below, including what the behavior is and how it makes you feel.

Brainstorm ways you can set a boundary for each. What do you need them to do or stop doing to protect yourself?

When you tell friends, family, and coworkers that you're working on yourself and need them to respect your new boundaries, you want to focus on yourself and your needs and make your request without sounding judgmental, in a manner that will also elicit their support.

Practice what you will say to communicate what has been bothering you and how you want it to change.

Even when you're clear, people will forget to honor your boundaries. It's up to you to enforce and reinforce them. How will you enforce and reinforce your new boundaries?

"FOCUS ON THE FACT THAT YOU'RE DOING YOURSELF A FAVOR RATHER THAN FEELING LIKE YOU'RE DENYING YOURSELF SOMETHING . . . THINK ABOUT ALL THE PLUSES OF PARTICIPATING IN YOUR NEW HABIT, WRITE THEM DOWN, AND NOTICE WHAT A GREAT FRIEND YOU'RE BEING TO YOURSELF."

Jen Sincero
Badass Habits

Be Patient

Resetting habits takes mental focus, time, persistence, dedication, and repetition. Expecting quick results that will last isn't realistic. One way to establish patience is to recognize that, even if you haven't yet achieved the desired result, every action you take towards resetting your habit is working 'underground' in your brain and psyche. Try to see each repetition you achieve as a step in the right direction. Keep at it, and after a few weeks, you'll see some improvement; and if you consciously choose to repeat the new habit long enough, eventually the impulse to slide backwards or even quit will subside, and the new habit will become something you automatically do, without having to think about it.

How many 'steps in the right direction' have you made recently? What can you do to celebrate your progress and reward yourself?

"KARMA ISN'T COSMIC.
IT'S YOUR HABITS CATCHING UP."

James Clear
Atomic Habits

What Stage Are You In?

Resetting habits has a series of stages. Knowing where you are can help you persist. Here's the four primary stages:

CONTEMPLATION: "I'm thinking about it."

You might be in this stage if you:

- ❑ have been considering change but are not quite ready to start
- ❑ believe that your health, energy level, or overall well-being will improve if you develop new habits
- ❑ are not sure how you will overcome the roadblocks that may keep you from starting to change

PREPARATION: "I have made up my mind to take action."

You might be in this stage if you:

- ❑ have decided that you are going to change and are ready to take action
- ❑ have set some specific goals that you would like to meet
- ❑ are getting ready to put your plan into action

ACTION: "I have started to make changes."

You might be in this stage if you:

- ❑ have been making eating, physical activity, and other behavior changes in the last six months or so
- ❑ are adjusting to how it feels to eat healthier, be more active, and make other changes such as getting more sleep or reducing screen time
- ❑ have been trying to overcome things that sometimes block your success

MAINTENANCE: "I have a new routine."

You might be in this stage if:

- ❑ your changes have become a normal part of your routine
- ❑ you have found creative ways to stick with your routine
- ❑ you have had slip-ups and setbacks but have been able to get past them and make progress

Whatever stage you are in, set yourself up for success and keep forging ahead.

Skip Those New Year's Resolutions

In a two-year study (1988) that examined the rate (people succeed at upholding their New Year's resolutions, researchers Norcross and Vangarelli found that 77 percent of resolution-makers honored those pledges for one week. However, only 19 percent of them kept their resolutions after two years. If this statistic is indicative of habits in general, at least eight times out of ten, you are more likely to fall back into your old habits and patterns than you are to stick with a new behavior.

Practice Radical Self-Compassion

Most of us set our expectations too high and then punish ourselves when we can't meet them. When resetting habits, you both need and want to both set reasonable expectations and hold yourself accountable, but offering yourself compassion when you get off track will improve your chances of getting back on track. If this is hard for you, think of it a radical self-compassion as a strategy for strengthening motivation.

What are five ways you could offer yourself radical self-compassion?

1. ______________________________

____

____

2. ______________________________

____

____

3. ______________________________

____

____

4. ______________________________

____

____

5. ______________________________

____

____

"THE COGNITIVE REVOLUTION LED PEOPLE TO FOCUS ON MOTIVATION, GOALS, COGNITIVE PRACTICES, HOW PEOPLE THINK. BUT WE'RE FINALLY SEEING THE LIMITS OF THOUGHTS AND FEELINGS, AND WE'RE STARTING, AS A DISCIPLINE, TO REALIZE THAT HOW PEOPLE ACTUALLY ACT DAY IN, DAY OUT IS ALSO QUITE IMPORTANT."

Wendy Wood, Ph.D.

Good Habits, Bad Habits: The Science of Making Positive Changes That Stick

Reframe Your Identity

As discussed in Chapter 1, your self is the autobiographical part of you that takes form based on your experiences, your choices, and your actions. It's how you think about yourself and determine whom you wish to be in the world. Every time the urge strikes remind yourself that you are no longer the person who scarfs down sugary treats and that you are now the person who either finds something else to do or opts for healthy snacks, like apples.

When you see new behaviors as a crucial part of whom you wish to be, it will reinforce the repetition required to ingrain the habits. Effectively, this desired identity can drive your new behavior. You can both think of and see yourself in a new light, as in "I am someone who no longer procrastinates. I am someone who tackles new projects with a plan and achieves them one step at a time."

How would you like to reframe your identity? Write three descriptions by first addressing the behavior you are changing (the five habits you want to reset) and then concluding with the new identity you will form because of successfully resetting the habit.

Habit #1: ____________________

Old identity ____________________

New Identity ____________________

Habit #2: ______________________________

Old identity ______________________________

____

____

____

____

____

____

____

____

____

____

New Identity ______________________________

____

____

____

____

____

____

____

____

____

Habit #3: ____________________

Old identity ____________________

New Identity ____________________

Habit #4: ____________________

Old identity ____________________

New Identity ____________________

Habit #5: ______________________________

Old identity ______________________________

New Identity ______________________________

Link it to Your Values

Core values are the root beliefs and meaningful perspectives that guide your behavior towards yourself and with others. We generally form our core beliefs in childhood, which is why it's always good to review them and contemplate which have become the ones currently driving how you make decisions and live your life.

Also, when you link any habits, you want to create to the values that matter most to. you, it provides motivation and strength for going forward. To get you started thinking about values, here's a list of common core values. Circle or highlight any that hold the most meaning to you.

Commitment to family and community	Harmony	Self-discipline
Love of self and others	Honesty	Spiritual practices
Having a Mission in Life	Introspection/Self-Compassion	Responsibility
Nurturance	Leadership	Loyalty
Exploration	Risk Taking	Tradition
Excellence	Courage	Nature preservation
Mastery	Justice	Creativity

Achievement	Fairness	Adventure
Faith	Resilience	Altruism

Are there core values you hold that are not in the chart? If so, list them, then pause to contemplate why they're important and how they could both shape and reinforce the habits you wish to create.

The core values that inspire and drive my behavior are:

Are the five habits you want to reset not in alignment with your core values? If so, how can you this to motivate the actions needed to ingrain the new habits?

Do the five habits you want to reset reflect who you are or who you used to be?

How do the five new 'replacement' habits reflect who you want to be?

"THERE ARE ONLY THREE THINGS WE CAN DO THAT WILL CREATE LASTING CHANGE: HAVE AN EPIPHANY, CHANGE OUR ENVIRONMENT, OR CHANGE OUR HABITS IN TINY WAYS."

BJ Fogg

How do your desired new 'replacement' habits specifically serve at least three of your values?

Can you link each replacement habit to other values that are important? Which ones and how do they reinforce each?

"HABIT IS HABIT AND NOT TO BE FLUNG OUT OF THE WINDOW BY ANY MAN, BUT COAXED DOWNSTAIRS A STEP AT A TIME."

Mark Twain

Seven Habits to Adopt

Seven highly desirable habits that could vastly improve your mental, emotional, physical, and spiritual health are:

1. **Mindful mornings:** Start your day by drinking a glass of water, don't automatically check your phone or start scrolling.
2. **Daily movement:** Walk every day (mindfully, in daylight if possible) and find other activities that will help you maintain a healthy weight and keep your body strong and flexible.
3. **Consistent learning:** Make time in your life to keep learning new things; read every day or study philosophy.
4. **Gratitude/goal reflection:** Write down one thing you're grateful in your life; take a few minutes every day to reflect on your goals.
5. **Healthy eating:** Choose foods that will nourish your body and keep your brain functioning at peak level.
6. **Setting boundaries:** Boundaries make time and space for you to pursue your goals, make yourself a priority, and prevent others from upsetting you or bringing you down.
7. **Prioritizing sleep:** Healthy sleep habits provide a foundation of well-being and productivity. While you sleep, your brain processes everything that happened to you that day and clears the deck for the next day.

The key is consistency, starting small, and then building on these habits to foster personal growth and success.

Which of the 'highly desirable' habits do you need to address?

____

____

____

How could you start small and build momentum?

Make a commitment here to add at least one of 'highly desirable' habits.

The Magic of Threes

Some have found that spending three minutes a day focused on practicing a new habit, as a means of providing three small wins a day (morning, afternoon, evening), for a period of three-weeks is the minimum requirement before stacking another new habit.

Use a Ten-Minute Rule

This is a simple strategy for breaking 'bad' habits, though it's not always easy to accomplish. When a craving or impulse to succumb to a habit you're trying to reset arises, promise yourself that you'll wait ten minutes between the time the urge strikes and the action you typically take. Often that 'waiting period' is enough to counteract the desire. You could always do a few yoga poses, meditate for ten minutes, write in your journal, or listen to motivational songs.

Think of five things you could do for ten minutes to stave off the impulse to repeat the habit you're attempting to reset?

1. ______________________________

____

2. ______________________________

____

3. ______________________________

____

4. ______________________________

____

5. ______________________________

____

"YOU CANNOT EXPECT TO ATTAIN SUCCESS IF YOU ARE NOT PREPARED. LIFE HAS A HABIT OF GIVING BACK REWARDS IN PROPORTION TO THE EFFORT WE EXPEND."

Catherine Pulsifer

Prepare for 'If Then' Situations

This strategy is about preparation for those situations when you struggle to reset the habit and fall short of your goals. Everyone slips at some point, and it's important that you have a planned strategy for how you'll quickly get back on the desired track.

Examples: If I am craving a donut, I'll eat an apple instead. If I reach for my cell phone to start doom scrolling, I'll read a scintillating novel instead. I know I'm going to be exhausted, hungry, and lazy when I get home, so instead of overeating or eating something unhealthy, I'm going to stop on my way home to buy a salad and fruit.

What habits will likely put you in an 'if then' situation? List them and replacement habits you can use to stay on track.

If ______________________________

____

Then I Will ______________________________

____

If ______________________________

____

Then I Will ______________________________

____

If ______________________________

____

Then I Will ______________________________

____

If ____

____

Then I Will ____

____

If ____

____

Then I Will ____

____

If ____

____

Then I Will ____

____

Create a Viable Plan

This is where you apply rubber to the road: create a workable plan that you will put into action!

After making your plan, start by setting realistic goals for putting your plan into action. Remember that it can take more than two months to reset a habit, and that it's often beneficial to start with small changes. For example, you can commit to walking around a block three times a week. Then, once that's become an autopilot habit, you can up the ante by increasing the time, distance, the frequency, or the intensity of your walk.

For Success: Set SMART Goals

Because it's not easy to reset habits and make the change permanent, it's essential that you make what you want to achieve doable. To facilitate success, set SMART goals. Here's what that means:

SPECIFIC

For example, if your goal is to eat healthier: Start small, like cutting back on sugar for four out of seven days a week. Buy and stock healthy alternatives to make it easier to reset.

MEASURABLE

If there's no way to track your progress, your brain won't be getting the dopamine hit it craves. Create a system for tracking what you're doing and the impact it is having. This will also help you make any adjustments needed.

ATTAINABLE

If you set your goals too high, you are setting yourself up for failure. Make the goals something you can achieve. You can also progress from easier goals to achieve to more difficult ones.

RELEVANT

Make sure that the habit reset is pertinent to what you're trying to achieve.

TIMELY

Charing your progress, not only bolsters motivation (and dopamine hits!), but it also helps you identify any weaknesses and quickly make adjustments.

Key benefits of developing good habits include:

- ❑ **Improved Physical and Mental Health:** Regularly exercising and eating healthily improves your sense of well-being, reduces stress, and lowers the risk of chronic disease.
- ❑ **Greater Efficiency and Productivity:** Healthy and productive habits remove the need to make constant decisions, freeing up mental space and energy.
- ❑ **Long-Term Goal Achievement:** Small, consistent actions sustained over time become building blocks that bridge the gap between where you are and where you want to be.
- ❑ **Stability and Consistency:** When healthy habits become ingrained routines, it brings structure to your daily life and provides a sense of control even when you're are under stress or anxious.
- ❑ **Increased Self-Discipline and Confidence:** Consistently following through on positive behaviors can vastly increase your self-esteem and strengthen your commitment to your personal well-being.

The Many Benefits of Resetting

Curbing nonproductive or unhealthy habits and replacing them with productive and healthy habits has been shown to automate positive behaviors, reduce mental effort and stress, and foster long-term health, productivity, and goal achievement. When you create and adhere to new routines, you strengthen your willpower, increase self-control, and create lasting, sustainable life improvements. Habits turn daily actions into automatic, compoundable progress.

Work Habits Reset Strategy

Many of us struggle to change our working. habits and to maintain momentum over time, thus creating an action plan is key to avoiding potential pitfalls. Here are eight tips for setting the kinds of habit reset goals that will help you maintain momentum:

1. **Make The Goal Concrete:** If you make your goals too abstract, it's hard to know where to start and how much emphasis to put on various stages. Break larger goals down into more manageable steps that can be achieved with specific actions. Instead of making your goal 'making sure I'm better prepared,' make it 'spend 30 minutes at the end of each day to strategize for the next day.' This more specific framing will make it easier to set the habit in motion, and to evaluate your progress.
2. **Identify the Requirements:** Each goal will require different parameters to achieve it. To add exercise, for example, the plan should include parameters like what days, for how long, and what activities you want to do so you don't have to figure it out each time. Creating specific plans also reduces the amount of mental energy required and makes the process of achieving your goal as painless and easy as possible.
3. **Set Aside Time:** Instead of waiting for an opportunity to arise, reserve the appropriate amount of time in your calendar so you can make sure other events don't interfere with the time commitment you're making to establish your new habit.
4. **Personalize Your Approach:** Some people thrive best when seeking to accomplish a goal all at once while others find more success in taking things step-by-step. Maybe you love to start on Mondays, or the first day of a new month, or your birthday. Maybe you need small steps that slowly lead to the most challenging change. Maybe you have a unique way of approaching habit resets. Whatever it is, make it yours.

5. **Make a social commitment:** Close friends, social groups, and coworkers can offer a huge assist. Having opportunities to discuss challenges and celebrate successes can bolster your spirit along the way and thereby keep you motivated and on track. You can likely find online groups who are working on similar challenges.
6. **Celebrate successes:** As you make progress, make sure to acknowledge your successes and the work it's taken to get there. Celebrating not only gives you the credit you've earned but also is a reminder that you have the wherewithal to achieve your goals, no matter where you are in the process.
7. **Be realistic:** Whether your goal is focused on changing old habits or building new ones, both can have their challenges. Mistakes and setbacks can happen and it's important to be compassionate toward yourself. Focus on progress not perfection or a hard deadline. If you have a day where you don't achieve your goal, re-commit for the next occasion.
8. **Course Correct if Needed:** You may realize your initial goal was too ambitious, and you need to course-correct or revise that goal while still working toward your long-term objective. Determination is important, but having the judgment to make these decisions as you go may serve you better in the long run.

Which of the strategies you listed will you use to reset your work habits and how will you implement each?

Why Good Work Habits Matter

Good work habits, when consistently practiced, generate performance and contribute to job satisfaction and richer relationships. When you cultivate self-awareness, it enables you to channel your natural talents towards positive habits that support your goals.

By aligning your daily actions with your unique strengths, you can experience the numerous benefits of overcoming bad habits, such as increased productivity, reduced stress, and a greater sense of fulfillment. Here are a few science-supported benefits after you break bad work habits:

- ❏ You keep distractions to a minimum.
- ❏ You achieve the level of 'deep work' that will help you become more engaged in your work.
- ❏ You make use of time productively.
- ❏ You encourage goodwill in coworkers and bosses.
- ❏ You clear your mind to be able to focus on your current tasks instead of trying to multitask throughout the workday.
- ❏ You feel more comfortable at work. The chances of achieving job success and getting promoted will increase.

Describe your current work habits. Which do you think need improvement?

Using what you've learned, what could you do to improve your work habits?

What outcomes do you hope to see once you've improved your work habits?

How do you think your improved work habits will improve the rest of your life?

Adopting Productive Work Habits

For every change you desire to make—whether it's to rearrange your daily agenda so you can get more accomplished, prioritize your days so you can meet your goals, change from slow and disorganized to organized and efficient, you'll be likelier to succeed if you figure out what specific, recurring problems are holding you back.

You may have very specific habits you need to reset at work, and hopefully, you can use the methods we've already discussed in depth to work on those, as well. In case you need any suggestions, the followin are all aimed at increasing productivity at work.

MAINTAIN A POSITIVE ATTITUDE

The time you most need a positive attitude is when you are tackling challenging tasks. If you feel bogged down and discouraged, do something to lift your mood. Take a five-minute break to practice deep breathing. When you return to work, adopt a steady pace and pause occasionally to notice how well you're progressing.

CREATE A SCHEDULE

Creating a 'to-do list' is always efficient, but once you have the list, break it down into specifics steps, then order it according to what you can get done easily and what will require more time and greater focus, then create a schedule, allotting time for the tasks that must get done.

FOCUS ON ONE TASK AT A TIME

It's almost impossible to do anything well if your brain is not clearly focused on the task at hand. Once you have the schedule of tasks and the amount of time you'll spend on each, make sure to keep your brain trained on one task at a time.

GIVE YOURSELF A LONG LEAD TIME

Once you have a project that you know will take a significant amount of time, over a period of days or weeks, jump right in. If you procrastinate, the pressure will build and you're less likely to perform at the level you desire. Also, create a gameplan for getting it done on time.

FIND YOUR MOST PRODUCTIVE TIME

If you're all fired up in the morning, tackle the work that will require the most time and focus. Or, if you're better after lunch, work on smaller tasks in the morning. The point is to take full advantage of what you know is the time of day you are most alert and productive.

REWARD YOURSELF AFTER TASKS

When you're establishing new, more productive habits, rewarding yourself is a very important part of the process. It doesn't have to be a big reward (or food), just do something that recognizes your accomplishment. Call a friend, send an email, take a short walk, or simply sit at your desk and deep breath for a few minutes—just acknowledge that you're doing it as a reward.

Resetting Productivity

A bad work habit is a recurring negative behavior or pattern that disrupts productivity, diminishes job performance, and can harm professional relationships. These habits often develop over time and can stem from poor time management, lack of organization, or ineffective communication skills. Identifying and addressing the bad work habits that are holding you back is crucial for achieving long-term career success. Twenty-three examples of nonproductive work habits are:

Procrastination

Poor communication

Multitasking

Tardiness

Negativity

Being disorganized

Distractions

Taking frequent breaks

Complaining

Negative attitude

Smartphone use

Dressing unprofessionally

Skipping lunch

Working while sick

Abusing privileges

Avoiding feedback

Avoiding technology

Checking emails constantly

Leaving your schedule to chance

Lying

Missing deadlines

Being unhygienic

Being too talkative

"I NEVER COULD HAVE DONE WHAT I HAVE DONE WITHOUT THE HABITS OF PUNCTUALITY, ORDER, AND DILIGENCE, WITHOUT THE DETERMINATION TO CONCENTRATE MYSELF ON ONE SUBJECT AT A TIME."

Charles Dickens

Thinking back to the five work habits you identified about, what obstacles might you face in resetting your habits, and how will you work around them?

Habit #1

Habit #2

Habit #3

Habit #4

Habit #5

"REMIND YOURSELF THAT YOUR REAL LIFE IS HERE IN YOUR PHYSICAL SURROUNDINGS AND TALKING TO PEOPLE AND DOING THINGS. MAKE SOCIAL MEDIA SOMEWHERE YOU GO INSTEAD OF THE PLACE YOU LIVE."

Oliver Burkeman,
Four Thousand Weeks

Digital Detoxing Increases Productivity

In today's modern world, they started as a massive convenience, but now all of us are too attached to our cell phones, tablets, and/or computers. While they're essential to both our work life and our personal life, being constantly available or spending more time on your phone than you do talking to coworkers, friends, or family the more your mental health suffers.

According to a March 2025 CBS News report, excessive cell phone (or tablet) use alters the brain, making users less attentive and more prone to mental health struggles. Even worse, excessive, mindless scrolling (nine+ hours a day) leads to decreased focus, inability to pay attention, and symptoms of 'brain rot' or addictions, similar to drug addiction.

Excessive cell phone use is also associated with reduced sleep quality which leads to less restorative sleep, daytime fatigue, and cognitive impairments, and research also shows that smartphone dependence contributes to family conflict and lessens face-to-face interaction.

Experts recommend developing analog hobbies that will keep you away from a digital screen. You can also establish healthy habits that will help you limit the amount of time you spend attached to your cell phone or on screens. Below are suggestions for healthy detoxing habits you can adopt or adapt:

- ❑ Turn off social media notifications, as they are rarely so important they need your immediate attention.
- ❑ Set boundaries at work that you won't accept work calls or texts after a certain hour, unless it's an emergency.
- ❑ If you aren't expecting your boss or another 'emergency' text, obviously you may want to keep notifications on, but if that's not the case and you still can't imagine turning your notifications off, try leaving them on but don't pick up your phone and automatically look at them. Wait at least 15 minutes, then keep increasing the time to 30 minutes, 45 minutes, an hour.

- ❏ When you come home after work, set your phone somewhere and leave it there. Only pick it up if you receive a phone call. Do not pick it up to scroll.
- ❏ Give yourself 30 minutes a day to scroll social media, break it up into two 15-minute sessions.

Are your cell phone habits productive or nonproductive, or even harmful? What do you struggle with most?

____

____

____

____

____

____

____

What steps are you willing to take to digitally detox?

____

____

____

____

____

____

____

The Confrontation: ADMITTING THE TRUTH BEHIND YOUR HABITS

Changing habits is always a challenge, and work habits can prove even harder to reset. When you get stuck, it's important that you confront your conscious or unconscious excuses for failing to change. Take each of the five habits you want to reset and answer the following questions:

HABIT #1

The Shadow Question: What is this nonproductive habit currently protecting me from? (e.g., Does my procrastination secretly protect me from an unconscious fear of being judged on my work? Was I frequently criticized as a child, or in school? Am I hesitant to start new projects because I expect to fail?)

The Cost Analysis: How does continuing the habit hold me back? If I don't change this habit today, what will my finances, and career progression look like three years from now? Be brutally specific.

The Secondary Gain: What hidden (not obvious, perhaps unconscious) reward do I get from this nonproductive habit? Is it comfort, distraction, a sense of control, an excuse to fail? How can I address the underlying problem?

The Identity Check: Does this habit align with the person I claim to be, or is it a relic of a person I used to be? Remember that resetting your identity is part of the habit reset process. Do I need to adjust how I think about myself at work? How much have I grown?

The Honest Mirror: If a coworker or a person I deeply care about adopted this exact habit, would I be worried for them? Why? What specifically would concern you and how would you express your concern? How would recommend they reset their habit?

HABIT #2

The Shadow Question: What is this nonproductive habit currently protecting me from? (e.g., Does my procrastination secretly protect me from an unconscious fear of being judged on my work? Was I frequently criticized as a child, or in school? Am I hesitant to start new projects because I expect to fail?)

____

____

____

____

The Cost Analysis: How does continuing the habit hold me back? If I don't change this habit today, what will my finances, and career progression look like three years from now? Be brutally specific.

____

____

____

____

The Secondary Gain: What hidden (not obvious, perhaps unconscious) reward do I get from this nonproductive habit? Is it comfort, distraction, a sense of control, an excuse to fail? How can I address the underlying problem?

____

____

____

The Identity Check: Does this habit align with the person I claim to be, or is it a relic of a person I used to be? Remember that resetting your identity is part of the habit reset process. Do I need to adjust how I think about myself at work? How much have I grown?

The Honest Mirror: If a coworker or a person I deeply care about adopted this exact habit, would I be worried for them? Why? What specifically would concern you and how would you express your concern? How would recommend they reset their habit?

HABIT #3

The Shadow Question: What is this nonproductive habit currently protecting me from? (e.g., Does my procrastination secretly protect me from an unconscious fear of being judged on my work? Was I frequently criticized as a child, or in school? Am I hesitant to start new projects because I expect to fail?)

The Cost Analysis: How does continuing the habit hold me back? If I don't change this habit today, what will my finances, and career progression look like three years from now? Be brutally specific.

The Secondary Gain: What hidden (not obvious, perhaps unconscious) reward do I get from this nonproductive habit? Is it comfort, distraction, a sense of control, an excuse to fail? How can I address the underlying problem?

____

____

____

____

____

The Identity Check: Does this habit align with the person I claim to be, or is it a relic of a person I used to be? Remember that resetting your identity is part of the habit reset process. Do I need to adjust how I think about myself at work? How much have I grown?

____

____

____

____

____

The Honest Mirror: If a coworker or a person I deeply care about adopted this exact habit, would I be worried for them? Why? What specifically would concern you and how would you express your concern? How would recommend they reset their habit?

____

____

____

HABIT #4

The Shadow Question: What is this nonproductive habit currently protecting me from? (e.g., Does my procrastination secretly protect me from an unconscious fear of being judged on my work? Was I frequently criticized as a child, or in school? Am I hesitant to start new projects because I expect to fail?)

The Cost Analysis: How does continuing the habit hold me back? If I don't change this habit today, what will my finances, and career progression look like three years from now? Be brutally specific.

The Secondary Gain: What hidden (not obvious, perhaps unconscious) reward do I get from this nonproductive habit? Is it comfort, distraction, a sense of control, an excuse to fail? How can I address the underlying problem?

The Identity Check: Does this habit align with the person I claim to be, or is it a relic of a person I used to be? Remember that resetting your identity is part of the habit reset process. Do I need to adjust how I think about myself at work? How much have I grown?

The Honest Mirror: If a coworker or a person I deeply care about adopted this exact habit, would I be worried for them? Why? What specifically would concern you and how would you express your concern? How would recommend they reset their habit?

HABIT #5

The Shadow Question: What is this nonproductive habit currently protecting me from? (e.g., Does my procrastination secretly protect me from an unconscious fear of being judged on my work? Was I frequently criticized as a child, or in school? Am I hesitant to start new projects because I expect to fail?)

The Cost Analysis: How does continuing the habit hold me back? If I don't change this habit today, what will my finances, and career progression look like three years from now? Be brutally specific.

The Secondary Gain: What hidden (not obvious, perhaps unconscious) reward do I get from this nonproductive habit? Is it comfort, distraction, a sense of control, an excuse to fail? How can I address the underlying problem?

___

___

___

___

___

The Identity Check: Does this habit align with the person I claim to be, or is it a relic of a person I used to be? Remember that resetting your identity is part of the habit reset process. Do I need to adjust how I think about myself at work? How much have I grown?

___

___

___

___

___

The Honest Mirror: If a coworker or a person I deeply care about adopted this exact habit, would I be worried for them? Why? What specifically would concern you and how would you express your concern? How would recommend they reset their habit?

___

___

___

A Final Note on Habit Reset

When you've eradicated your 'bad' habits and created and ingrained so many positive habits that you don't even have to think about them anymore, your self-esteem and confidence will dramatically rise. What you are doing becomes automatic, which means you do it without thinking. You also don't have to rely on willpower or motivation, which what separates those who develop productive and healthy habits from people whose bad habits limit their ability to achieve theirs.

SIXTEEN TIPS FOR PERMANENTLY RESETTING HABITS

Learning about habits is an integral part of the empowerment process. It's important to know ways to integrate good habits or extinguish bad habits. Here's a recap of sixteen strategies you can use to reset your habits:

1. **Do something simple and achievable every day** until it becomes automatic. Even after conscious motivation decreases, once a habit is formed, less focus, conscious motivation, and effort are needed, which makes the habit far more likely to continue. This is why habits are useful—once they become automatic, they take less mental energy.

2. **Heighten motivation by starting small** and gradually building up to bigger tasks and goals.

3. **Make the cues easy to recognize.** When looking to create a habit, choose an easy context cue (e.g., after breakfast, just before bed, when you finish the dishes, etc.).

4. **Set goals you can meet,** and review and reset them to keep momentum.

5. **Specify what is motivating the reset.** When you're clear on why you want to change a habit, it's helps you stay on track.

6. **Be persistent.** Until the new habit becomes automatic, you're likely to feel discomfort and will have to exert more self-control. Be prepared to stay strong.

7. **Be patient.** Understand that more complex behaviors will take longer to extinguish or adopt than easier behaviors. Give yourself more leeway when complex habits are being addressed.

8. **Weather setbacks.** Realize that you will backslide and find it harder to self-regulate or put in the effort required to reset your habits. This is normal. Don't use it as an excuse to quit. Push past it and keep going.

9. **Reward progress.** Our sensory nervous system is continuously monitoring which actions satisfy our desires and deliver pleasure. For good habits, this substantiates the need to consistently return and reinforce the rewards, which help you to create and sustain the habit. For bad habits, understanding your habit loop and the pleasurable sensations it evokes can help you extinguish habits that don't serve you well.

10. **Don't rely on intention.** Evidence has shown that as the strength of a habit grows, intention becomes decreasingly predictive of the behavior. All the ongoing processes for habit reset that take place in your brain (production of dopamine, memory and consolidated learning, associations it makes) it's not enough to rely on intention. You have to consciously and proactively commit to incrementally doing things differently than you had before.

11. **Make whatever changes in lifestyle that will support your efforts.** To change or break a habit, you must create the environment in which it will be easier to prompt good behaviors and increase friction to make bad habits inconvenient.

12. **Don't go it alone.** For accountability and to sustain interest and motivation, enlist support from family members, friends, or someone else who's encouraging.

13. **Use mindfulness for mental strengthening.** To help break unproductive habits, use mindfulness to turn toward experiences rather than away from them. Let it help you learn to gradually sit with discomfort in service of doing what you want to be doing.

14. **Foster curiosity, reflection, and personal insight.** It forges an openness to new habits and decisions that will help to break habit loops leading you to more mindful actions.

15. **Connect your habit resets to your values.** To create continual motivation and fuel the creation and sustaining of habits, identify your purpose or personal meaning to connect the desired new behaviors (or those you want to extinguish) directly to your values.

16. **Give yourself credit.** Learn the art of self-compassion and self-love. Believe in yourself and identify opportunities to boost your self-esteem.

Good luck on your habit resetting journey!

"SOW AN ACT AND YOU REAP A HABIT.
SOW A HABIT AND YOU REAP A CHARACTER.
SOW A CHARACTER AND YOU REAP A DESTINY."

Charles Reade

Resources

Badass Habits: Cultivate the Confidence, Boundaries, and Know-How to Upgrade Your Life, Jen Sincero, Penguin Random House, New York, 2021.

Habits for Healing: Reclaim Your Purpose, Peace, and Power, Nakeia Homer, Penguin Random House, New York, 2024.

Hello, Habits: A Minimalist's Guide to a Better Life, Fumio Sasaki, W. W. Norton, New York, 2021.

Level Up: Your Mental Toughness Boot Camp, 100 Exercises to Boost Your Resilience, Determination, and Grit!, Michelle Ribeiro, Adams Media, Avon, MA, 2021.

Rising Strong: How the Ability to Reset Transforms the Way We Live, Love, Parent, and Lead. Brene Brown, Ph.D., LMSW, Random House, New York, 2027.

Train Your Brain to Get Happy: The Simple Program that Primes Your Gray Cells for Joy, Optimism, and Serenity, Adams Media, Avon, MA, 2011.

You Don't Have to Change Everything: Six Ways to Shift Your Vantage Point, Stop Striving for Happy, and Find True Well-Being, Beth Kurland, Ph.D., Health Communications, Boca Raton, 2024.